The Inspiring Wisdom
of Viktor E. Frankl

THE
Inspiring
Wisdom
OF
Viktor
E. Frankl

A 21-Day Reflection
Book About Meaning

Pam Roy & Moira Hummel

VFIA
VIKTOR FRANKL INSTITUTE
OF AMERICA PUBLISHING

VFIA Publishing
Los Angeles, CA

Cataloging-in-Publication Data is on file with the Library of Congress

Paperback ISBN: 978-1-7348862-0-7
e-book ISBN: 978-1-7348862-1-4

Interior design by Amy Hayes Design
Editorial and self-publishing guidance by knliterary.com

ViktorFranklAmerica.com

Printed in the United States of America

From Pam

For my daughters, Emily, Rachel, and Allison, and youth
everywhere yearning to discover meaning in their lives.

From Moira

For Brian, Becky, Joe, Tori, Jessica, Noah, Kathy, and my
parents with many thanks for your love and support.

CONTENTS

CONTENTS

Many people are familiar with the name of my grandfather, Viktor Frankl, but few know much about his message. He is often recalled as a Holocaust survivor, but in reality, that experience played a small role in his overall life's work. His greatest contribution to humanity was recognizing meaning as a central factor in mental health.

My grandfather's interest in psychology started at an early age. He enrolled in adult night classes when he was in junior high school. His first article was published when he was eighteen, and by the time he was twenty-two, he was lecturing on the meaning of life. In 1930, at the age of twenty-five, he organized youth counseling centers in Vienna, successfully combatting the epidemic of teen suicides that would occur around the time report cards were issued. Within a year, suicides dropped to zero. By the time he completed medical school, he had developed a specialty in psychiatry and neurology with a focus on treating suicidal patients.

His views about meaning brought him into conflict with Sigmund Freud and Alfred Adler, the founders of modern psychotherapy. As a teenager, he corresponded with Freud, and then joined Adler's school for a time. While my grandfather acknowledged the importance of their work, he went on to establish his own theory, which is often referred to as the third Viennese school of psychotherapy. He named the theory Logotherapy, from the Greek for "healing through meaning."

Years before World War II, he treated thousands of suicidal patients at psychiatric hospitals and developed the core principles of Logotherapy. The completed manuscript of his first book about it was confiscated when he was sent to Auschwitz. He was thirty-seven years old at the time. His encounters with the worst of human conditions ended up providing him with an unwanted laboratory that confirmed his theory. He saw that those who were oriented toward a meaning to be fulfilled were more likely to survive.

After the war, he taught throughout the United States and held professorships at Harvard, Stanford, Southern Methodist University, and Duquesne University in Pittsburgh. The English translation of his book *Man's Search for Meaning* was published in 1959 and became an international bestseller. My grandfather saw this not so much as a personal achievement, but as a symptom of the mass neurosis of modern time since its title promised to deal with the question of life's meaningfulness. Decades later, the book still shows up consistently on Amazon's top 100 books.

Logotherapy as a psychological practice is hard to standardize, package, and market, so it has not gained as much traction in the United States as it has in other parts of the world. It recognizes that every person is unique and cannot fit into a standardized theory. Requiring creativity and flexibility, therapy at its best is as much an art as a science. He liked to refer to American neurologist George M. Beard, who noted that if two cases of neuroses were treated the same way, at least one was treated improperly.

I was lucky enough to grow up knowing my grandfather both personally and professionally. He encouraged my love of filmmaking when I was a teenager and also supported my decision to become a Logotherapist when I was an adult. I have had the privilege to archive innumerable videos and interviews of him throughout his life. These are constant reminders of his timeless wisdom and his wonderful sense of humor—another quality he believed to be a resource of healing and well-being.

I met Pam and Moira while we were working together on a film project. Friends for over forty years, they were inspired to write this thought-provoking book about meaning because of their concern for America's youth and the growing epidemic of mental illness. They recognize the importance of my grandfather's philosophy of life and have used it to guide their own lives and raise their children. Just as he did, they see the bigger picture, the underlying problems, and the systemic issues that need to be addressed. My grandfather would be pleased that they are introducing his ideas to a new generation of readers.

—*Alexander Vesely*

INTRODUCTION

"People may have enough to live by;
but more often than not they do not
have anything to live for."[1]

As human beings, we are motivated to find meaning.
However, meaning is unique to each person. It cannot be
created or given to us—it must be discovered. Our search
for meaning is a personal journey that each of us must
take. This book facilitates that journey. Through inspiring
quotes from Viktor Frankl and accompanying exercises
for self-discovery, it offers twenty-one reflections on
topics such as purpose, freedom, and self-transcendence.
These reflections can be contemplated over twenty-one
days or twenty-one years. They can be done in any order
and revisited at any time. They simply create space for you
to become more aware of who you are and how you fit
into the world. Life has meaning under all circumstances,
including the most undesirable. Even if our only source
of meaning is our attitude toward an unavoidable
situation, we have the freedom and responsibility to
answer the demands life presents to us. No matter where
you are in your life, this book facilitates the search for
meaning, which is our primary motivation for living.

The life and work of Viktor E. Frankl (1905–1997)
inspired this book. From the time he was a young
boy, Frankl believed that meaning was central to life.

As a neurologist and psychiatrist, he studied it. As a philosopher, he sought to understand it. As a survivor of concentration camps during the Holocaust, he lived it. Frankl's life journey showed him that "he who has a *why* to live can bear almost any *how*." This quote by Friedrich Nietzsche anchored Frankl's belief that discovering our *why*—the meaning we attach to our lives—is essential to our health and well-being.

Before the onset of World War II, Frankl had developed a theory called Logotherapy, which literally means "healing through meaning." His extensive university training, combined with his experiences working in suicide clinics and living in concentration camps, reinforced his theory. While Logotherapy is a form of psychotherapy (part of humanistic and existential psychology), it is also a philosophy for life, focusing on meaning, freedom, and responsibility. For the purposes of this book, we use its guidance as a life philosophy rather than its clinical application.

Over a nine-day period following the war, Frankl wrote his bestselling book, *Man's Search for Meaning*. Based on a 1991 survey by the Library of Congress, the book was considered "one of the ten most influential books in America." The first part of the book describes the horrors of the Holocaust when Frankl lost his parents, his brother, his wife, and his unborn child. The second part introduces and explains Logotherapy, which focuses on what is right with us, our humanity and our meaningful futures. *Man's Search for Meaning* has inspired millions around the world.

Logotherapy recognizes the interrelationship of the mind, body, and spirit. It teaches that there is a human spirit alive and well in each one of us. This spirit gives us the ability to step outside ourselves and reflect on our lives, provides us with goals and direction, and generates freedom of choice. It is what distinguishes us from other mammals—not falling under the umbrella of any religion, but instead representing the essence of our humanness. Our human spirit is always healthy and has vast untapped resources. When we ignore or suppress it, we can become distressed. Throughout time, the defiant power of our human spirit has inspired our evolution. It is constantly striving to push us forward, from who we are to what we can become.

When our search for meaning is denied, thwarted, or ignored, we experience an inner void that Frankl termed an "existential vacuum." It is this vacuum that produces anxiety, depression, aggression, addiction, and even suicide. We can see the telltale signs of this existential vacuum everywhere in our culture, affecting all ages, races, and socioeconomic levels. Every era has its own collective neurosis, and this existential vacuum is ours.

Like all humans at any time, we want to avoid the suffering caused by guilt, pain, and death—the "tragic triad" that Frankl explains is part of being human. For Frankl, suffering is not the same as despair—despair is suffering without meaning. Suffering is unavoidable. Despair involves choice. Indeed, our resistance to examining our suffering for meaning leads to despair, which in part, results in the epidemic levels of self-harm, addiction, mental illness, and suicide.

Our culture's current focus on the pursuit of happiness is actually one of the causes of our existential vacuum and feelings of despair. We feel ashamed if we are unhappy, as if it were a disease. It is not possible to be happy all the time; it is an unattainable goal. Life brings with it some unavoidable, unhappy experiences. The choices we make and how we deal with these times give our lives meaning and, thus, fulfillment. Frankl's work shifts our focus away from the naïve pursuit of happiness to the mature pursuit of meaning.

As you will discover through the reflections to come, meaning is all around us and available to us at any moment. It can be found through:

- making a difference in the world through our actions, our work, or our creations;
- experiencing something (truth, beauty) or encountering someone (love); and
- adopting a courageous and exemplary attitude in situations of unavoidable suffering.

As humans, we are characterized by our spirituality, our freedom, and our responsibility. But too often, we choose not to take responsibility for ourselves. We want someone else to be responsible for us, to provide us with certainty in an uncertain world. We like to turn over responsibility to corporations, governments, schools, churches, and even medical professionals. But finding and fulfilling meaning is our personal task, not something we can delegate.

Each of us is unique and irreplaceable. That existential

void we feel is real and an affliction of our time. However, reaching into that void to discover meaning will free us to become who we are meant to be. The philosophy of Logotherapy teaches responsibility as the cornerstone of freedom. It seeks to prevent spiritual distress and the resulting mental illnesses with a focus toward the future and our unique role in shaping it. Most of all, Logotherapy encourages us toward self-transcendence, the ability to share our authentic self with others to better a worthy cause or to love another. This is the highest goal of human beings, and it has the power to change the world.

"A human being is not one thing among others; things are determining each other, but man is ultimately self-determining ... After all, man is that being who has invented the gas chambers of Auschwitz; however, he is also that being who has entered those gas chambers upright, with the Lord's Prayer or the Shema Yisrael on his lips."[2]

Purpose

"A man* who becomes conscious of the responsibility he bears toward a human being who affectionately waits for him, or to an unfinished work, will never be able to throw away his life. He knows the 'why' for his existence, and will be able to bear almost any 'how.'"[3]

We need to know we matter in the world, that there is a place for our uniqueness, and that what we have to offer cannot be offered by anyone else. When we believe we are no more valuable than a manufactured widget, suicide can feel like a reasonable option. This feeling of despair happens when we lose sight of our distinct contribution to the tapestry of life.

Mark Twain said, "The two most important days of our life are the day we are born and the day we figure out why." We are invaluable to the world—we all have a purpose for being here. Purpose is something we discover, and for each person it is different. We can find it only in the context of our lives—through our contributions, our relationships, our experiences, and

*Befitting the era of his writing, Viktor Frankl used "man" to refer to humankind—it is not related to gender.

our attitudes. Purpose is not about tallying up individual achievements. Purpose is about consciously forging our own path. When we are able to see the many meaningful moments we create and experience, whether they are big or small, we will not throw away our life. We recognize our significance and importance.

Reflect on your relationships, your contributions, or your experiences in the last month. Identify one or more instances where your presence made a difference, big or small. What unique characteristics or contributions did you make? How did your presence make a difference?

THE INSPIRING WISDOM OF VIKTOR E. FRANKL

Living

"A life of short duration ... could be
so rich in joy and love that it could
contain more meaning than a life
lasting eighty years."[4]

There is a difference between living and existing.

Existing is traveling through life on autopilot. Existing
is ignoring our conscience. Existing is wanting to be
told what to do by people or institutions or conventions.
When we are existing, we are not thinking about our
actions. We are following others for a sense of belonging
and identity. We plod through the drudgery of life,
missing out on embracing the present moment rather
than choosing to connect to causes, experiences, and
people that can give our lives meaning.

Living is embracing life in all its messy glory. Living
is recognizing what is and adapting to change. Living
is being responsible for the things we can control and
looking to transcend ourselves to connect with others.
When we are living, we are making choices every
moment of every day and realizing that those choices
have consequences—good and bad. Sometimes we find
ourselves in situations that are outside our control, and

even in these circumstances there is meaning to be found. Ultimately, living is about finding the meaning in all circumstances and responding to what life is demanding of us. It is the difference between sitting in the boat and drifting versus taking up the oars and rowing as best we can.

Are you living or existing? What can you do
to live life more fully?

THE INSPIRING WISDOM OF VIKTOR E. FRANKL

Happiness

"Happiness must ensue. It cannot
be pursued. It is the very pursuit of
happiness that thwarts happiness.
The more one makes happiness an aim,
the more he misses the aim."[5]

Everyone says they want to be happy. We wish it for
our loved ones and ourselves. Harvard's and Yale's
curriculums now offer classes on happiness. According to
Yale, it is the most popular class in the school's history.

Frankl reminds us that while we think we want to be
happy, what we really want is a reason to be happy.

When we make happiness the goal, we establish an
unattainable expectation. Happiness, in and of itself,
is not a sustainable emotion because life has ups and
downs. Catastrophes, disappointments, and conflicts are
as much a part of life as prosperity, success, and harmony.

Frankl describes happiness as a side effect of finding
meaning or purpose in life. Happiness occurs when we
are least focused on ourselves. It follows in the wake
of those times when we give of ourselves to a cause we
believe in or to the love of another. Happiness is the
reward that ensues when we do something meaningful.

Reflect on a moment when you experienced great happiness. What were you doing? Was your focus on yourself or something else? What were the reasons that moment made you happy?

Reactions

"An abnormal reaction to an abnormal situation is normal behavior."[6]

We often find ourselves focusing on the "abnormal reaction" our mind or body is exhibiting (anxiety, depression, headaches, stomachaches, self-harm, addiction), but such pathologizing fails to put our experiences into context. Often the reaction is completely understandable given the situation.

Our painful reactions are signals that something is not right. Depression is normal when we regularly compare ourselves and our lives to the seemingly perfect bodies and perfect lifestyles we see on social media. Chronic anxiety is normal in the face of constant performance testing, being bombarded with negative news, and answering to relentless deadlines set by others. Often these signals relate to the repression of our spirit's pursuit of meaning or the devaluation of our uniqueness in favor of one-size-fits-all approaches.

We are never free from conditions, but we are free to take a stand, either in the choices we make to change the condition or, when that is not possible, in our attitude toward it.

Reflect on an "abnormal reaction" you are having, perhaps anxiety or depression. What is the situation you are in? What specifically about the situation is contributing to your reaction? Can you change the situation? If not, how can you change your attitude? Does the change in attitude or situation modify your reaction?

Tolerance

"Being tolerant does not mean that I share another one's belief. But it does mean that I acknowledge another one's right to believe, and obey, his own conscience."[7]

Each one of us is unique—even within our own families, cultures, and religions. While as human beings we are more alike than different, we must acknowledge these differences and the right of other people to have different beliefs and views. The context of our individual lives shapes us, and we can never truly put ourselves in another's shoes. We must try and learn to respect their viewpoint and engage in healthy discourse. It is only when we seek to understand rather than to be understood that we are able to expand our perspectives.

Since tolerance is built on understanding not judging, seek out someone who holds a view contrary to your own and ask them to explain their position. Rather than thinking about your rebuttal, listen carefully so you can summarize their position in a way that they believe accurately reflects their views. You can begin your summary with, "I'm hearing you say that ..." and then ask if this is correct. Ask if they would be willing to reciprocate the practice with you. What did you notice about the experience of listening carefully? About being heard?

THE INSPIRING WISDOM OF VIKTOR E. FRANKL

Community

"The meaning of individuality comes
to fulfillment in the community. To this
extent, then, the value of the individual
is dependent upon the community. But if
the community itself is to have meaning,
it cannot dispense with the individuality
of the individuals that make it up."[8]

The Masai warriors in Africa greet each other as follows:

"How are the children?"
"All the children are well."

The Masai know that the strength of their community is
only as good as the health and well-being of the weakest
and most dependent members, usually the children. In
every society, children reflect the health of the adults and
the community overall.

Our children are not well. On one end, our culture leaves
countless children behind in under-resourced schools
and communities. On the other end, we place a relentless
focus on resume building for college applications. Either
way, our children are left with little time to develop a
sense of self, explore interests, and invest in relationships.

Across the board, standardized education and its tests devalue the uniqueness of each human being and miss the multiple levels of human intelligence. This, combined with our children's dependence on social media for validation and personal connection, has undermined their ability to develop a sense of significance and belonging within their communities. Of course, this affects us all. For the first time, we have disbanded our human tribe and are going it alone, which leaves us feeling isolated even in the midst of a sea of humanity.

Human beings need connection, collaboration, and cooperation to flourish. It is how we grow and develop. We need to recognize and respect the relationship between the health of the individuals who make up our communities and the health of our society as a whole, especially our most vulnerable members, like our children.

Reflect on your role in one of the many communities in which you belong (for example, family, work, church, neighborhood, or city). How does your involvement support your connection to others? Could your connections to others help you grow as an individual and enhance your community?

Self-Transcendence

"Being human means always being directed toward something other than oneself. Even the concept of self-actualization can never do full justice to the main essence of human existence ... Human existence is not characterized by self-actualization but rather by what I call self-transcendence— pointing beyond itself."[9]

No man is an island. We are all interconnected, and it is only through others that we become truly fulfilled human beings. This is why self-actualization, by itself, is not enough to help us reach our potential. Self-actualization focuses solely on the improvement of the individual—with the goal of perfecting our *self*. According to Frankl, this is too limiting. His core belief was that self-transcendence—reaching out beyond ourselves—was the ultimate goal of our existence. We are profoundly social beings, and our lives require interconnection.

Over the course of history, we have been inspired by the unselfish actions of people who have stepped up to address the challenges and needs of their time. Mother Teresa left the comfort of a wealthy family to dedicate herself to those in extreme poverty. On September 11, 2001, as the World Trade Center was burning and collapsing, firefighters and police officers ran up the stairwells to help save those trapped inside. During the global pandemic of 2020, medical professionals, active and retired, made similar sacrifices in the face of exposure to a deadly virus. All these actions epitomize self-transcendence.

The transformative power of moving beyond ourselves is where we find deep satisfaction. This comes from knowing that our lives matter and that we each have an important role to play in improving our world.

Reflect on your goals and aspirations. Do they involve something or someone other than yourself? How might you modify them to reach self-transcendence? What are a few immediate changes you could make to expand your focus?

THE INSPIRING WISDOM OF VIKTOR E. FRANKL

Be the Change

"But, the human being is responsible and free and is responsible for his own behavior and conduct and decisions and always retains the freedom to change."[10]

When we stand on the sidelines and critique, without participating in the solution, we usually end up angry and frustrated because we have made ourselves powerless. It is important to remember that we always have the ability to change ourselves, which in turn gives us the power to change our world.

For example, when we decide to improve our health by walking more, going to the gym, or joining a hiking club, we not only improve our physical well-being, but we also change our attitude about ourselves, meet new people, and sometimes inspire someone we care about to do the same.

On a broader scale, if we are mad about the harm being done to the environment, we can engage in activities that benefit the environment. A positive reaction to problems not only changes our personal world but also the world in general.

We have the ability to choose to change ourselves and address the things, big or small, that we don't like in our lives and our world. Instead of delegating responsibility to other people or institutions and then becoming frustrated with them for not solving the problems that concern us, we can follow Gandhi's advice and be the change we wish to see in the world.

Identify a personal or world issue you are concerned about and then identify a change you can make (for at least three weeks) that will help to address the issue. After three weeks, note how your changed attitude or behavior impacted you, those around you, the issue itself, and also your belief in your power to change yourself and your world.

Humor

"One might say as well, that humor helps man rise above his own predicament by looking at himself in a more detached way. So humor would also have to be located in the noetic dimension. After all, no animal is able to laugh, least of all at himself."[11]

As we engage with life, we encounter hurtful and embarrassing moments that cause us to be self-critical or feel shame. We can handle this by becoming cautious and limiting our exposure to moments of failure, or we can follow Frankl's advice and use our human ability to detach from ourselves with humor and gain perspective. The problem with the first approach is that when we limit our exposure, we also limit our potential—and our ability to experience the full range of life's joys and opportunities. Viewing our life with humor is essential to accepting our imperfections and coping with life's uncomfortable situations. Laughing at our low moments encourages us to forgive ourselves and allows us the vulnerability we need to deeply connect with others.

Talented comedians are excellent observers of the human condition and turn universally embarrassing moments into shared moments of laughter. Often the people we enjoy most are those who can laugh at their own mistakes or flaws and allow other people to laugh with them. We connect more through our imperfections than our perfections. When we develop our uniquely human skill of self-distancing with humor, we are able to maximize our potential and enjoy life.

Reflect on an embarrassing moment in your life. Step back and put it in perspective. Turn it into a funny story. Tell it to yourself. Tell it to someone else. Notice how it feels to use humor to heal.

Uniqueness

"The meaning of life must be conceived in terms of the specific meaning of a personal life in a given situation. Each man is unique, after all, and each man's life is singular; no one is replaceable nor is his life repeatable."[12]

We are so much more than the combined DNA of our parents or products of our environment. We are each as distinct as our fingerprints; even identical twins have different fingerprints!

Every one of us has something to contribute to the world. Our contributions do not stem solely from our perfections, but also from our imperfections. A 2019 study showed 35 percent of US entrepreneurs are dyslexic. Dyslexia, classified as a learning disability, is in fact what gives these entrepreneurs their unique ability to problem solve—they see the world in a different light.

What makes us unique and different is often what gives us an advantage. Our distinct makeup is comprised of our talents and flaws, our strengths and weaknesses, as well as our experiences, whether they are positive or negative. All these things make us unique and irreplaceable.

Consider what makes you unique. What do you view as your talents, strengths, and positive experiences? What do you view as your handicaps, weaknesses, and challenging experiences? In what ways can you use your unique characteristics and experiences to help others or causes you care about?

THE INSPIRING WISDOM OF VIKTOR E. FRANKL

Humanity

"There [are] a lot of tasks in wait for us all. We would just have to make another step after having arrived and developed what is called monotheism, the belief in one God. We should also obtain what I would like to call 'monoanthropism' the awareness of one mankind. A unity of mankind which goes beyond all different colors, be it colors of the skin or colors of the various political parties."[13]

While we are all individuals, we also share a common humanity. At certain moments in time, we are especially aware of this. When Neil Armstrong first stepped on the moon, the world stopped to watch in awe as he proclaimed, "That's one small step for man, one giant leap for mankind." It was a unifying moment of joy. Similarly, pandemics, mass murders, and natural disasters unite us in grief and sorrow. It is in these moments that we recognize each other as fellow human beings and are able to focus more on our commonalities than our differences.

We share the same planet. Wars and strife in one region generate migration patterns that affect other regions;

disease and pollution in one part of the world eventually travel to other parts of the world. Caring for each other and our planet is essential to our health and well-being. What happens to one of us eventually affects us all.

When we step outside ourselves and choose to get involved, we often discover what we have in common with the people we want to support and causes we want to assist. When we shift our focus from ourselves to the world around us, we often find contentment, fulfillment, and purpose.

Think of someone that you feel is very different from yourself (maybe even the same person you spoke with for reflection five) and identify views and/or values that you have in common. How does this shift your opinion of that person? What actions might flow from this broadened perspective?

THE INSPIRING WISDOM OF VIKTOR E. FRANKL

Freedom

"I do not forget any good deed done to me, and I carry no grudge for a bad one."[14]

If anyone had a reason to carry a grudge, it would have been Viktor Frankl. He was the survivor of four Nazi concentration camps and lost his parents, brother, wife, and unborn child in the Holocaust. Despite these horrific events, he chose not to be consumed by hatred and blame.

Logotherapy focuses on choice, even if it is only the choice of the attitude we take in a situation of unavoidable suffering. Sadly, tragedy can befall anyone at any time. It can present itself in the form of wars, crimes, or disease. Our freedom comes in how we respond to each personal crisis that confronts us. By identifying as victims, we are prevented from identifying as survivors. To be controlled by anger and to insist on blame renders us powerless. When we consciously choose how we respond, we regain control and power over our future. We cannot change the past. We can only learn from it and decide who we want to be as we responsibly move forward.

Is there a situation in your life that makes you feel like a victim or trapped by your fears? Can you retell the story to yourself, casting yourself as courageous, empowered, or as a survivor? How does it feel to play that role? Moving forward, what thoughts and actions will allow you to shift the focus from "what was" to "what will be"?

THE INSPIRING WISDOM OF VIKTOR E. FRANKL

Money

"We all know the type ... who is entirely
devoted to earning money, who is so
busy earning the means for living that he
forgets life itself. The pursuit of wealth
has become an end in itself. That kind of
person has a great deal of money, and
his money still has a use, but his life no
longer has a direction. In such a person
livelihood overshadows life."[15]

Frankl uses the term "will to money" to refer to the
focus on the pursuit of money as the primary driver of
a person's life. Our culture reveres the wealthy. We view
wealth as the solution to all problems and as the creator
of status, belonging, and respect. Our corporations and
our education systems make upward financial mobility
the goal.

It is not money itself that is the problem, as it can
actually make a positive impact in the world. The issue is
how we view money and what we do with it. If we focus
on acquiring wealth beyond our basic needs, it can lose
its value of enhancing our life by consuming our time
and energy. Money can buy things, but it cannot buy
love, happiness, or fulfillment.

Our society encourages us to live our lives according to what author David Brooks calls "résumé virtues"—accomplishments and financial rewards that we feel set us apart from everyone else. But study after study shows that it is our "eulogy virtues"—deep relationships, community contributions, and meaningful work—that we are most remembered for and that give us fulfillment in life.

Keep a log for a week, noting how you spend your time (sleep, work, friends, significant others, family, hobbies, and so forth). Are you spending time on the things you value and want to be remembered for? If not, what shifts could you make in time and/or attention to focus on eulogy virtues?

Emptiness

"Let me just quote from a letter I recently received from a young American student: 'I am a 22-year-old with degree, car, security, and the availability of more sex and power than I need. Now I have only to explain to myself what it all means.' However, such people are complaining not only of a sense of meaninglessness but also of emptiness, and that is why I have described this condition in terms of the 'existential vacuum.'"[16]

Frankl expressed concern over our mechanistic education system, noting that people are not machines and that to treat them as such would lead to an existential vacuum (feeling of emptiness) resulting in depression, aggression, and addiction. As early as 1928, he developed counseling centers for students in Vienna who were committing suicide around the time report cards were issued. Frankl got the students to identify meaningful goals for their future rather than hyperfocusing on their immediate academic performance. The suicide rate dropped.

The education system seeks to conform students to an external standard that is often not meaningful to them, resulting in boredom (lack of interest) and apathy (lack of motivation). Even after people complete their schooling, the pattern of pursuing goals set by others continues—meeting career goals set by employers, commitment expectations set by community and religious organizations, as well as social expectations set by peers. These externally imposed benchmarks often overwhelm us, leaving us with little time to think about or pursue things that matter to us.

When we ignore our individuality and our need to discover our unique meaning and purpose for living, we are left feeling empty. By critically evaluating whether or not external benchmarks are in line with our personal values and goals, we are empowered to live a meaningful life.

Are you hyperfocused on your performance, or do you feel empty inside? If so, identify at least one personal goal you can work toward that will positively impact your life.

THE INSPIRING WISDOM OF VIKTOR E. FRANKL

Responsibility

"While we enjoy freedom, it may well be that we are not yet sufficiently aware of our responsibility. If we were, we would soon find that there is plenty of meaning and purpose lying in wait for us all. Just think of the underprivileged parts of the world, of the underdeveloped people and nations. Think of the needs and opportunities. Think of man's planet-wide responsibilities, and no one will ever have to complain of lack of meaning or lack of purpose."[17]

Our ability to choose what we do in life is what gives us our freedom. Frankl repeatedly emphasized that we are not free from conditions, but we are always free to choose how we respond to them. Because we are free, we are responsible for who we become and how we address the issues that impact our families, communities, and the world.

Although we cannot control the limitations that biology and circumstances place on us, we can decide how they will influence our lives. What makes us unique is also what makes us uniquely capable of improving situations or the lives of others. We must put our energy, talent, and experience toward positively contributing to the issues that call to us, whether that means curing diseases, helping foster youth, or solving world hunger. It is only when we recognize that our freedom comes with responsibility that we can improve the quality of our lives and the state of the world. Life doesn't just happen to us. As Frankl says, we have to play an active role in making life meaningful.

Exercise the freedom that comes with responsibility by looking at any problem of concern to you (personal, communal, or global) and identifying at least two ways that you can respond. After noting the likely outcomes and how they align with your values, decide how to respond. How does consciously deciding how to respond make you feel?

THE INSPIRING WISDOM OF VIKTOR E. FRANKL

Human Spirit

"Man's search for a meaning is not pathological, but rather the surest sign of being truly human. Even if this search is frustrated, it cannot be considered a sign of disease. It is spiritual distress, not mental disease."[18]

Our human spirit is never sick. It can become distressed and manifest itself outwardly in ailments that affect our bodies and/or minds. We often want to see these things as psychological or biological problems so we can label them with a diagnosis and attempt to find a cure. This approach reduces us to only a mind and body and ignores the spiritual dimension that is the essence of our humanity.

Our spiritual dimension is what provides us with the resources and strength we need to move forward in our lives. These resources include:

- our ability to learn from our mistakes, allowing us to adapt to new circumstances;
- our sense of humor, putting our failings into perspective;
- our conscience, giving us the ability to take a stand for things we believe in or against things we think are wrong;

- our ability to love others, helping us move beyond ourselves; and,
- our passion for a cause, allowing us the potential to create change in the world.

The search for meaning is a deeply personal and spiritual journey. No person or system can determine what is meaningful for us or define what will give our lives purpose. Because our culture is driven by external benchmarks (wealth, power, individual achievement, everlasting youth, physical perfection) that keep us perpetually busy, we often find ourselves on a treadmill that robs us of the time and energy required to discover what life is asking of our human spirit. We need to look at whether what we call *disease* (or *dis*-ease) is really our spirit crying out in distress.

Is your body or mind signaling something to you?
Rather than a psychological or biological issue,
could this signal be related to the suppression of
your human spirit? If you had to guess, what is
your spirit longing for?

THE INSPIRING WISDOM OF VIKTOR E. FRANKL

Tension

"Thus, it can be seen that mental health is based on a certain degree of tension, the tension between what one has already achieved and what one still ought to accomplish, or the gap between what one is and what one should become. Such a tension is inherent in the human being and therefore is indispensable to mental well-being."[19]

In order to grow and change, we need tension between what we are and what we want to become. While we might desire equilibrium in our body (with sleep and nutrition) and our mind (with stable emotions), it is not always healthy for our spirit. When equilibrium is the goal, we are likely to stick with what is comfortable and familiar, thus limiting our opportunities for growth.

Tension has to be present in our spirit in order to propel us forward. Striving toward a goal, addressing the issues that arise in relationships, developing new skills, making new friends, and even falling in love can cause tension. All these things challenge our equilibrium. Luckily, our human spirit provides us with the resources we need to handle these situations. Only when we embrace the tension that comes with living can we fulfill our potential and become who we are meant to be.

Do you feel like you are struggling to reach a goal, create a project, or connect in a relationship? What is the tension between who you are and who you'd like to become? How can you turn this tension into fuel to help push you toward achieving your dreams?

THE INSPIRING WISDOM OF VIKTOR E. FRANKL

Solitude

"We need new types of leisure which allow for contemplation and meditation. To this end, man needs the courage to be lonely."[20]

The distractions of our modern society provide us with the opportunity to keep our minds occupied around the clock. Whether by streaming videos, checking emails, or engaging with social media, our busyness keeps us from listening to the human spirit within us—the conscience that guides us.

It is only when we slow down and reflect on our life that we can gain perspective. When we are alone and quiet, we can contemplate who we want to be and where we want to go. By contrast, when we are racing from one thing to another, keeping ourselves perpetually busy, we have to evaluate if we are running to something or from something. Often, we are running from loneliness; but loneliness is a part of being human. In fact, solitude is essential for reflecting on what matters to us and formulating our plans for the future.

As we go through life's inevitable ups and downs—with work or relationship transitions, social circle evolutions, and death of friends or loved ones—we experience loneliness. In our culture, loneliness can generate depression and anxiety, and often feels shameful. But we should also remember that loneliness is usually temporary and that it is during these periods of struggle that we grow the most.

Take a few minutes a day to sit with yourself.
You can use this time to contemplate or
meditate. This can be as simple as focusing on
your breath and quieting your mind. Note how
creating time for quiet solitude affects how you
feel and how you react to things.

THE INSPIRING WISDOM OF VIKTOR E. FRANKL

Suffering

"If there is a meaning in life at all, then there must be a meaning in suffering. Suffering is an ineradicable part of life, even as fate and death. Without suffering and death human life cannot be complete."[21]

While positive psychology certainly has its merits, it ignores suffering, which is an inescapable part of life. Psychologist Susan David calls this the "tyranny of positivity," as it creates an unrealistic expectation and generates shame when we have feelings that are not positive. Negative emotions are a natural part of being alive and allow us to experience the healthy range of human experience.

To experience great joy, we also must risk experiencing great pain. We must develop the ability to appreciate the highs and cope with the lows. When we run from suffering rather than accept the reality of its existence, we give it power over our lives and lose the opportunities for personal growth that it presents. To really live, we must be willing to experience the full range of emotions that come with being human.

What is your view of suffering? Is it something you avoid or accept? Looking back on a time of suffering, can you see personal growth that came from the situation? Based on this experience, identify healthy coping strategies you can use in the future.

Work

"The job at which one works is not what counts, but rather the manner in which one does the work. It does not lie with the occupation, but always with us, whether those elements ... which constitute the uniqueness of our existence are expressed in the work and thus make life meaningful."[22]

How work fits into our lives is largely dependent on how we view ourselves in relation to our job. When we disconnect our work from who we are and what we value, we lead a divided life. In this context of compartmentalization, the so-called work-life balance limits our potential to bring our unique contributions to all our interactions.

We have the freedom to choose how we invest ourselves in all aspects of our lives, including work. This allows us to find meaning in all that we do. If we view our work as an extension of our connection to inner meaning, work becomes integrated into our lives in a more profound way. The term work-life balance becomes more about time spent at different pursuits, not energy drained away from competing core pursuits.

For example, a nurse can strictly follow a doctor's medical orders, committing to procedure without engaging with a patient on an emotional level. Alternatively, the nurse can follow procedure while connecting with the patient through empathy and compassion. The second approach, where the nurse reaches out emotionally within the framework of expected duties, brings meaning through work.

Every occupation allows us to give of ourselves in a way that engages who we are, with our unique insights, understanding, genetics, and experiences. When these complex parts of our identities are put to work in a meaningful, purposeful way, we become indispensable and irreplaceable.

How does your work relate to your life?
Do you find it meaningful or does it help you
achieve personal goals? What aspects of who
you are and what you have experienced can you
incorporate into your work to make it
more meaningful?

Choices

"Death marking the end of a lifetime can frighten only the person who has not lived his lifetime to the full."[23]

Every day we are confronted with a multitude of demands and choices. The demands we meet and the choices we make will, over the course of our lives, define the type of person we are.

Viktor Frankl did not fear getting older or dying because he viewed life as an opportunity to do things that mattered and to consciously make choices that were meaningful. With each meaningful choice he built up a past that he could look back on with pleasure—a past that was permanently part of who he was.

If we take the time to think about how we want to be remembered, we might make totally different—and likely better—decisions about how to spend our time now. As we move forward in life, we are building a permanent past. By embracing the gift of each day and consciously engaging in the things we do, we can put the majority of our time and energy into things we consider important. Since we only live once, the choices we make matter.

Instead of making a bucket list of places to go and things to do, make a list of meaningful choices you have made and/or those you hope to make in the future.

ENDNOTES

INTRODUCTION

1. Viktor Frankl, *The Feeling of Meaninglessness* (Milwaukee: Marquette University Press, 2010), 203.

2. Ibid, 69.

REFLECTIONS

3. Viktor Frankl, *Man's Search for Meaning* (Boston: Beacon Press, 2006), 80.

4. Ibid, 117–118.

5. Viktor Frankl, *Man's Search for Ultimate Meaning* (New York: Perseus Publishing, 2000), 90.

6. *Man's Search for Meaning*, 20.

7. Viktor Frankl, *The Will to Meaning*, expanded ed. (New York: Plume, 2014), 46.

8. Viktor Frankl, *The Doctor and the Soul*, 2nd ed. (New York: Vintage Books, 1986), 71.

9. *The Feeling of Meaninglessness*, 144.

10. Viktor Frankl, "San Quentin Lecture," 1966.

11. *The Feeling of Meaninglessness*, 109–110.

12. Ibid, 119.

13. Viktor Frankl, "Youth in Search of Two Worlds Symposium," Sacramento State College Speech (audio tape), Frankl Family Archives, 1966.

14. Viktor Frankl, *Recollections: An Autobiography* (Massachusetts: Basic Books, June 2000), 35.

15. *The Doctor and the Soul*, 120.

16. *Man's Search for Ultimate Meaning*, 93.

17. Roots, John McCook, "A Human Dynamo Sparks US Colleges," *PACE Magazine*, 1967.

18. *The Feeling of Meaninglessness*, 49.

19. *Man's Search for Meaning*, 104–105.

20. *The Will to Meaning*, 73.

21. *Man's Search for Meaning*, 67.

22. *The Doctor and the Soul*, 118.

23. Ibid, 130.

SELECTED BIBLIOGRAPHY

Frankl, Viktor. *The Feeling of Meaninglessness*. Milwaukee: Marquette University Press, 2010.

———. *Man's Search for Meaning*. Boston: Beacon Press, 2006.

———. *Man's Search for Ultimate Meaning*. New York: Perseus Publishing, 2000.

———. *Recollections: An Autobiography*. Massachusetts: Basic Books, June 2000.

———. *The Doctor and the Soul*. 2nd ed. New York: Vintage Books, October 1986.

———. *The Will to Meaning*, expanded ed. New York: Plume, 2014.

———. San Quentin Lecture transcript, Frankl Family Archives, 1966.

———. Youth in Search of Two Worlds Symposium, Sacramento State College Speech (audio tape), Frankl Family Archives, 1966.

Roots, John McCook. "A Human Dynamo Sparks US Colleges." *PACE Magazine,* Los Angeles, 1967.

ACKNOWLEDGMENTS

This book would not have been possible without
the invaluable support, encouragement, and input
of Alexander Vesely, Viktor Frankl's grandson. As
a certified Logotherapist, he reviewed each draft to
make sure it stayed true to his grandfather's message.
Alexander and his father, Franz Vesely, provided us with
a multitude of resources from the family archives. We
are grateful to the Frankl family and the Viktor Frankl
Institute of Vienna for their indispensable assistance
with the creation of this book.

ABOUT THE AUTHORS

ABOUT PAM ROY

Pam is an advocate for the mental health and well-being of children and young adults. With her background in market research and business, she writes a blog, *Pam Roy Blog*, focusing on education and preparing students for both the future of work and a meaningful life. She is a mentor to youth making life decisions. She cohosts the podcast *Q-Ed UP with Ziz and Pam*, engaging in conversations about what it means to be educated in the twenty-first century.

Inspired by the meaning-centered philosophy of Viktor Frankl, Pam is involved in film and book projects related to bringing his ideas to a new generation. She is cofounder of the Viktor Frankl Institute of America and executive producer of the upcoming feature film, *Man's Search for Meaning*. She is also executive producer of *Meaning in Madness*, a soon-to-be released short film series which shines a light on the systemic issues contributing to the epidemic of mental health disorders in students. Pam is involved with nonprofit organizations helping foster youth as well as International Sanctuary, a social enterprise that empowers women escaping human trafficking. She is the mother of three adult daughters.

ABOUT MOIRA HUMMEL

Moira's career began as a civil litigation attorney specializing in research and writing. In 2015, she shifted her focus to pursuing her dream of working with children and young adults in foster care. For over a decade, Moira has worked with several nonprofits assisting foster youth at sibling reunification camps and in life-skills training programs. She has mentored and guided individual foster youth through life-changing events.

Additionally, Moira is the content editor for *Pam Roy Blog*, where she reviews posts and helps shape the arguments presented. For over fifteen years, she has been a volunteer and board member of Brothers' Helpers, a nonprofit feeding Los Angeles's homeless. Moira read *Man's Search for Meaning* and became convinced that Frankl's life philosophy has the potential to transform lives. She cofounded the Viktor Frankl Institute of America and is currently working on a program that will incorporate Viktor Frankl's teaching into her nonprofit work with foster youth. Moira is married to Brian and has three adult children and three grandchildren.

VIKTOR FRANKL INSTITUTE OF AMERICA

Learn more about the life and work of Viktor Frankl on our website. We offer resources and information about Viktor Frankl and Logotherapy, his meaning-centered approach to therapy and life. The website includes a personal biography, a summary of Logotherapy, video clips, books, films, and news articles.

Find us at:

VIKTORFRANKLAMERICA.COM

Want to join with others in discussing the book? Go to:

VIKTORFRANKLAMERICA.COM/INSPIRINGWISDOM

Additional resources can be found through
The Viktor Frankl Institute, Vienna:

VIKTORFRANKL.ORG

CPSIA information can be obtained
at www.ICGtesting.com
Printed in the USA
BVHW031202240222
630005BV00008B/339